Big
Science Ideas

What senses do animals have?

Bobbie Kalman
Crabtree Publishing Company
www.crabtreebooks.com

Big Science Ideas

Created by Bobbie Kalman

For my cousin Scott Brissenden,
an extraordinary young man,
with lots of love

Author and Editor-in-Chief
Bobbie Kalman

Research
Enlynne Paterson
Tammy Ovens

Editor
Kathy Middleton

Proofreader
Crystal Sikkens

Photo research
Bobbie Kalman
Crystal Sikkens

Design
Bobbie Kalman
Katherine Berti
Samantha Crabtree (cover)

Production coordinator
Katherine Berti

Illustrations
Tiffany Wybouw: page 27

Photographs
© Merlin D. Tuttle/Bat Conservation International: page 26
© Dreamstime.com: pages 17 (bottom left), 28
© iStockphoto.com: page 14 (bottom)
© Shutterstock.com: cover, pages 1, 3, 4, 5, 6, 7 (top), 8, 9, 10, 11, 12, 13, 14 (top), 15, 16,
    17 (top and bottom right), 18, 19, 20, 21, 22, 23, 24, 25, 27 (top), 29, 30, 31 (top)
Other images by Digital Stock, Digital Vision, and Eyewire

Library and Archives Canada Cataloguing in Publication

Kalman, Bobbie, 1947-
    What senses do animals have? / Bobbie Kalman.

(Big science ideas)
Includes index.
ISBN 978-0-7787-3285-3 (bound).--ISBN 978-0-7787-3305-8 (pbk.)

    1. Senses and sensation--Juvenile literature. I. Title. II. Series: Kalman,
Bobbie, 1947- . Big science ideas.

QP434.K36 2009   j573.8'7   C2009-901261-8

Library of Congress Cataloging-in-Publication Data

Kalman, Bobbie.
  What senses do animals have? / Bobbie Kalman.
      p. cm. -- (Big science ideas)
  Includes index.
  ISBN 978-0-7787-3305-8 (pbk. : alk. paper) -- ISBN 978-0-7787-3285-3
(reinforced library binding : alk. paper)
  1. Senses and sensation--Juvenile literature. 2. Animal behavior--
Juvenile literature. I. Title. II. Series.

QP434.K358 2009
573.8'7--dc22
                                                    2009008084

Crabtree Publishing Company

www.crabtreebooks.com   1-800-387-7650

Published in Canada
Crabtree Publishing
616 Welland Ave.
St. Catharines, Ontario
L2M 5V6

Published in the United States
Crabtree Publishing
PMB16A
350 Fifth Ave., Suite 3308
New York, NY 10118

Published in the United Kingdom
Crabtree Publishing
White Cross Mills
High Town, Lancaster
LA1 4XS

Published in Australia
Crabtree Publishing
386 Mt. Alexander Rd.
Ascot Vale (Melbourne)
VIC 3032

Contents

Our five senses

We have five senses. They are sight, hearing, smell, taste, and touch. Our senses help us make "sense" of our world.

Sense organs

Organs are body parts that do important jobs. Our eyes are organs that see colors, sizes, and shapes. Our ears pick up the sounds around us. Our noses smell the air or the scents of objects. They also help us taste. Our tongues and mouths tell us if our food is salty, sour, sweet, or bitter. Our sense of touch helps us feel the **texture** of objects. Are they soft, hard, scratchy, or sharp? Which senses are these girls using to paint their picture?

Good or bad?

How do you feel when you smell a flower, taste your favorite food, listen to music, touch a kitten, or see people you love? Your senses can make you feel happy, but they can also warn you of dangers!

Our sense of taste tells us if food is good to eat or if it might make us sick.

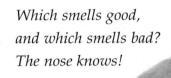

Which smells good, and which smells bad? The nose knows!

Hearing an angry dog bark and seeing it bare its teeth warns us to stay away or we might get hurt!

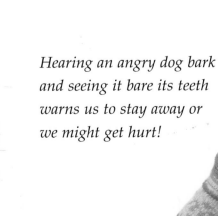

5

Do animals have senses?

Just like people, animals also need to get information about their world. Like us, most animals also have the senses of sight, hearing, smell, taste, and touch, but their senses may be very different from ours. For example, mice feel with their whiskers, and butterflies taste with their feet. Animals also use their senses in different ways than we do. For example, they use smell to find **mates**, to recognize animals in their groups, and to warn other animals to stay away!

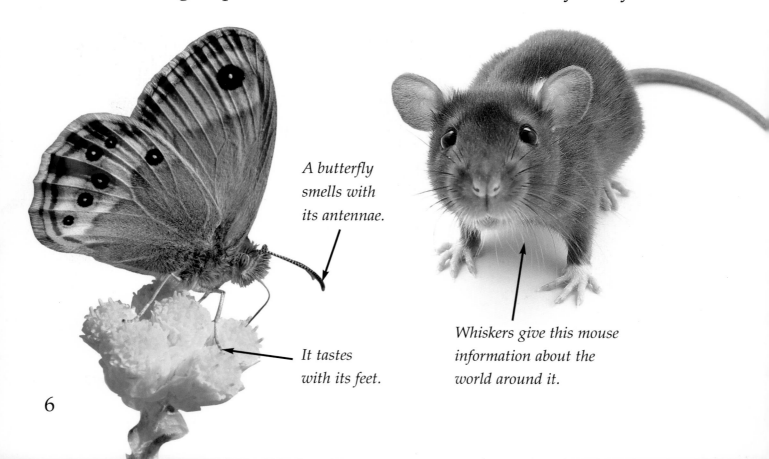

A butterfly smells with its antennae.

It tastes with its feet.

Whiskers give this mouse information about the world around it.

Staying alive!

Animals use their senses to find food and water, to travel from place to place, and to learn about dangers around them. They use their senses to **communicate** with other animals and protect their babies from **predators**. Predators hunt and eat other animals. Animals use their senses to stay alive!

It is winter, and the weather is cold. This monkey was bathing in a hot spring and got too warm. Which sense told the monkey to get out of the water?

These wolves are using their senses of hearing and smell to find animals to eat under the snow.

How do animals see?

The eyes of animals have **adapted**, or become suited, to the ways animals need to use them. Animals need to see so they can protect themselves and find food. Most animals have two eyes that can see size, shape, and color. They can also tell when something is moving. Some animals can see all the way around their bodies, some can see colors that we cannot see, and some see well in the dark. Some can see light and dark shapes, but not colors.

The eyes of owls are in the front of their faces. They look like human eyes. Owl eyes cannot move, but they can see better in the dark than our eyes can.

The eyes of hawks and eagles can see very far. From high in the sky, they can spot birds in the air or animals on the ground to hunt and eat. They grab the prey with their claws.

Animals that predators eat, such as deer, have eyes at the sides of their heads. Eyes in this position allow the animals to see predators around them, while they are looking for food.

Shiny eyes

Some animals have a **tapetum lucidum** layer at the back of their eyes. The tapetum helps them see better at night. It reflects light and makes the eyes of animals appear to glow in the dark. Dogs, cats, foxes, lemurs, raccoons, and some fish and birds have tapeta.

This flying lemur's eyes glow at night.

9

Different kinds of eyes

The eyes of animals come in several sizes, shapes, and colors. They can be in different places on the head. Some animals have two **simple** eyes. Simple eyes have one lens in each eye. Some animals have **compound** eyes. Some have both.

eye

A wolf spider has eight simple eyes.

Each of a chameleon's eyes can move in a different direction. This chameleon is looking up with one eye and down with the other.

Compound eyes

Insects have compound eyes. Compound eyes have many lenses. Each lens contains a tiny part of what an insect sees. The insect's brain then puts the parts together. Compound eyes see in many directions at the same time. They can see when something moves.

Dragonflies have huge compound eyes. Each eye has more than 30,000 lenses.

butterfly feeding

*Bees and butterflies can see **ultraviolet** colors that we cannot see. Ultraviolet colors and patterns guide them to the right kinds of flowers, where they will find food.*

11

Whose eyes are these?

Can you match these eyes to their owners? There are clues under each picture to help you guess. The eyes belong to a deer, fish, peacock, frog, moth, eagle, butterfly, chameleon, and cat. Two pairs of eyes are not real eyes. They are called **eyespots**. Eyespots frighten predators by making animals look bigger.

These eyes can see ultraviolet colors.

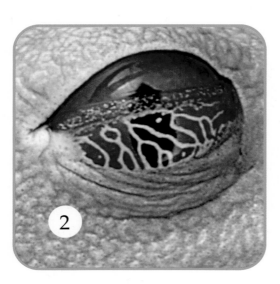

This animal closes two eyelids on each eye while it sleeps. Its third, clear eyelid protects its eyes while it is awake.

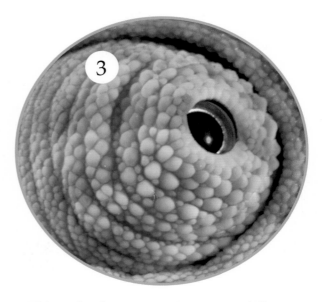

This animal can move its eyes in different directions. It can see all around itself.

These eyes see well under water.

This bird's eyes are not where they belong!

These eyes make this animal look scary.

This animal can see far below where it flies.

These eyes glow in the dark.

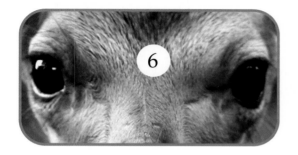

This animal's eyes are at the sides of its head.

The sense of smell

Many animals have a much stronger sense of smell than humans have. They use their sense of smell to find food, keep track of family, stay away from enemies, and find mates. Most **mammals** have a good sense of smell.

Dogs have an excellent sense of smell. They are often part of rescue units. Dogs can keep scents in their noses and follow them for a long time. They can even find people buried under deep snow.

How do they smell?

Humans and some animals have noses for smelling, but not all animals have noses. Insects smell with their antennae, and snakes pick up smells with their tongues. Fish have an excellent sense of smell, even though they are under water.

*A snake flicks out its tongue to pick up scents in the air. It then touches the tongue to the **Jacobson's organ** on the roof of its mouth. This organ sends the information to the snake's brain.*

Butterflies smell with their antennae.

nostrils

*Sharks are able to smell even a tiny bit of blood in ocean water. Just under their snouts, they have two nostrils. The shark sucks water into its nostrils to sniff out **prey**. Prey are animals that predators hunt.*

15

Scents sent

Many animals leave behind special scents called **pheromones**. These scents may be sprayed into the air, mixed with urine or saliva, or be rubbed onto objects. The scents may be used to warn other animals to stay out of a territory or to tell if an animal belongs to a family group. Animals also use scents to attract mates, with whom they can make babies. Bees and ants use scents to lead other members of their group to food.

When an ant has found food, it wipes its abdomen on the ground, leaving a tiny scent trail. The scent tells the other ants, "Food is this way!"

Prairie dogs greet one another with "kisses" that are not really kisses. These animals rub their teeth together to smell members of their group.

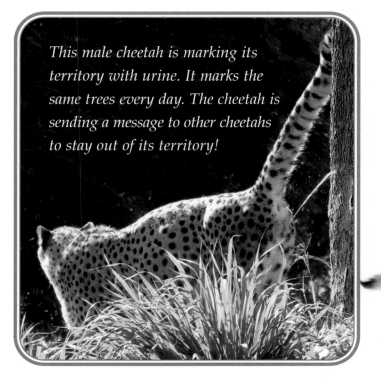

This male cheetah is marking its territory with urine. It marks the same trees every day. The cheetah is sending a message to other cheetahs to stay out of its territory!

This mother lynx is rubbing its scent on its baby. Cats have scent glands on both sides of their heads. The baby now has its mother's scent on its body.

Smell and taste

Pandas eat mainly bamboo.

We have only 9,000 taste buds, but rabbits have more than 17,000! They only eat plants.

The tongue is the main organ of taste. Much of the upper part of the tongue is covered in taste buds. Your tongue can tell you if something is sweet, sour, salty, bitter, or spicy. It can also tell you that food is delicious or that it tastes bad. We taste with our tongues, but our sense of smell makes our sense of taste much stronger!

Eating to live

Many animals smell and taste the way we do. People have favorite foods, but most animals eat only what their bodies need. For example, giant pandas eat almost nothing but bamboo. Animals eat to stay alive.

Pigs also have an excellent sense of smell. They use their noses to find buried food. Pigs have almost twice as many taste buds as humans have. These baby wild pigs have found food under the ground.

suckers

Octopuses touch and taste with the **suckers** on their tentacles. They can also stop other animals from smelling, as well as tasting, them! When an octopus is frightened, it squirts out a cloud of inky liquid. The ink confuses predators and takes away their sense of smell. The octopus can then get away.

Touching information

Touch tells this girl that the leaves of the pine tree are sharp!

For people, the main organ of touch is the skin. Our skin gives us information about whether objects are soft, sharp, rough, cold, hot, or heavy. We also use our fingers to touch and feel.

Touch and learn

Animals use their sense of touch to gather important information, which they need to stay alive. Touch helps them find their way in the dark, feel what is around them, and figure out what to eat. Touch helps animals avoid danger. Touch also allows animals to show that they care for one another. Just as we shake hands and hug, some animals also use touch to act friendly.

These monkeys are hugging each other and the kitten. They seem to like its soft fur.

Moles live under the ground. They have very small eyes hidden in their fur. Moles use mainly their senses of smell and touch. Their front feet are very large. Their palms are wide and have long fingers with sharp claws for digging. The mole finds its food by feeling through dirt for it.

Scorpions feel their way with the hairs on their legs and pincers.

Whiskers on cats and dogs help them keep their balance and find their way in the dark.

pincer

Hearing with ears

Hearing is the ability to pick up sounds using an organ such as an ear. The sounds travel to **eardrums** or other sound organs inside the body. These inner ears **vibrate**, or move back and forth quickly. The brain then figures out what the sound is. Many animals use sound to communicate, or send messages to one another. Hearing is very important to these animals. Birds use songs to let other birds know to stay out of their territories. Many animals also use hearing to find food or escape from predators.

Meerkats have excellent hearing. They use their hearing to find insects to eat. Meerkats also need good hearing to listen for warning calls. They take turns looking out for predators.

Elephants have excellent hearing. They hear with their big ears, but they also pick up sounds in the air with their trunks. They can use their feet to pick up vibrations in the ground, too.

Dogs can hear high sounds that we cannot hear. Cats can hear sounds that are even higher. Loud sounds hurt the ears of both of these animals.

Where are their ears?

Many animals have outer ears on the sides of their heads, but the ears of some animals do not look like ears. For example, lizards have openings at the sides of their heads, where sound enters. The eardrums of frogs look like big drums behind their eyes. These eardrums are called **tympanums**. Crickets, katydids, and grasshoppers have tympanums, too.

A katydid's tympanums are on its front legs. A tympanum senses vibrations.

tympanum

This lizard has ear openings. Sound enters through the openings and travels to the inner ear. Lizards cannot hear very well.

A frog's tympanum looks like a big drum.

25

What is echolocation?

Echolocation is creating sounds and then using their echoes to find and identify objects. It is a way of hearing and seeing with sound. Dolphins, some other whales, and insect-eating bats use echolocation.

Bats hunt at night. They use echolocation to help them "see" in the dark. The echoes tell bats where to find prey, such as flying insects. Echolocation also lets them know how big the prey is and in which direction it is moving. This bat caught a katydid using echolocation.

26

Where is the food?

Dolphins hear well through their lower jaws, but echolocation gives them more information about where to find food and what kind of food it is.

A dolphin sends out clicking sounds.

Echoes tell the dolphin about this fish.

These dolphins are using echolocation to find animals to eat under the sand at the bottom of the ocean.

Super senses

Some animals have more than the five senses of sight, smell, taste, hearing, and touch. Echolocation, used by bats and dolphins, is one of these extra senses. There are other senses, too. Some animals that live in water have **lateral lines**. A lateral line usually looks like a faint line running down the side of a fish from its head to tail. It is an organ that helps an animal feel movement, vibration, and changes in the water around it.

lateral line

The lateral lines on this shark run down both sides of its body, to the end of its tail.

Lateral lines help sharks locate prey. They may also give sharks a sense of direction in the ocean.

heat-sensing pit

Even in total darkness, some snakes can "see" and catch their prey. They use **infrared vision**. Two heat-sensing pits on their faces can feel the warmth given off by an animal's body. The pits on this rattlesnake's face can pick up even the tiniest bit of heat!

Some animals **migrate**, or move to a place far away and then back again. Sea turtles swim thousands of miles (kilometers) to lay eggs at the beaches where they hatched from eggs. They always know how to get there and back!

Birds, such as this migrating sand crane, may have built-in compasses that tell them in which direction they are flying. No one really knows how migrating animals find their way. They seem to use super senses!

Which sense is it?

This lemur looks for food at night. Which senses help it find food?

The animals on these two pages are using at least two of their senses. Match the animals to these senses:

1. hearing and echolocation
2. smelling, tasting, and ultraviolet vision
3. smell and touch
4. hearing and sight
5. night vision and smell
6. smell and infrared vision

This frog is using two senses. What are they?

Which two senses does this snake use to find food?

Horses use two senses when they greet each other. What are the two senses?

This butterfly is using its antennae, feet, and eyes. What senses are in these body parts? Which butterfly sense do we not have?

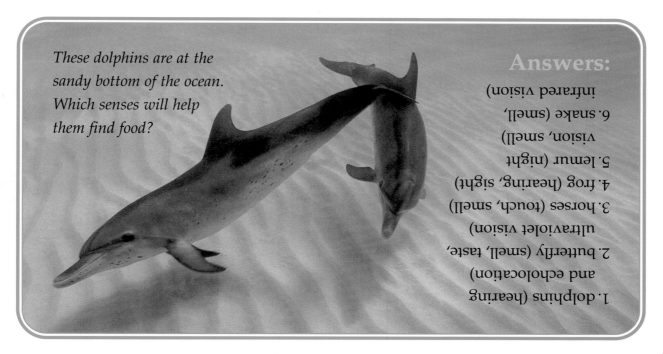

These dolphins are at the sandy bottom of the ocean. Which senses will help them find food?

Answers:

1. dolphins (hearing and echolocation)
2. butterfly (smell, taste, ultraviolet vision)
3. horses (touch, smell)
4. frog (hearing, sight)
5. lemur (night vision, smell)
6. snake (smell, infrared vision)

Glossary

Note: Some boldfaced words are defined where they appear in the book.

adapted Changed to suit a new purpose

communicate To pass along information through sounds and signals

echolocation The use of echoes to find and identify objects

eardrum A membrane in the ear that vibrates when it picks up sound and creates hearing

eyespot A marking on an animal that looks like an eye and confuses predators

Jacobson's organ An organ used for taste and smell, which is found on the roof of the mouth of some animals

lateral line A line of pores along both sides of the body of an animal that helps it sense vibration and pressure

mammal A warm-blooded animal that is born with hair or fur and drinks milk from its mother's body

mate A partner an animal needs to help it make babies

migrate To move to another area for a period of time and then back again

organ A part of the body, such as an eye or ear, which does an important job

pheromone A chemical that an animal releases to send messages to other animals

suckers Round disks on an octopus's arm that are used for touching, smelling, and tasting

texture The look and feel of the surface of something

ultraviolet A violet color not visible to humans

Index

Printed in the U.S.A.—BG